MAKING

Marriage

WORK

MAKING Marriage WORK

Margaret Grimer

GEOFFREY CHAPMAN
LONDON

A Geoffrey Chapman book published by
Cassell Publishers Limited
Artillery House, Artillery Row, London SW1P 1RT

First published 1987

ISBN 0 225 66494 1

British Library Cataloguing in Publication Data

Grimer, Margaret
    Making marriage work.
    1. Marriage — Religious aspects — Christianity
    I. Title
    261.8'3581   HQ734

Phototypeset by Scribe Design, Gillingham, Kent
Printed and bound in Great Britain by
Billing and Sons Limited, Worcester

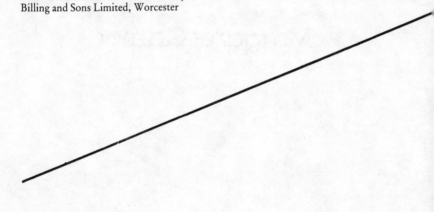

Contents

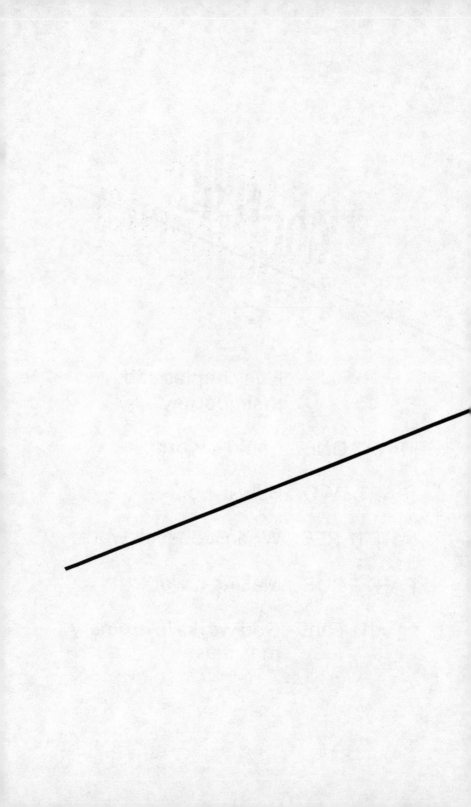

Five couples
and their journey

'I'd like our marriage to work—but will it?'

This book says that couples are not helpless in the face of marriage breakdown.

YOU can improve your chances of a successful and happy marriage

★ if you respect what each partner brings to the marriage

★ if you know how a married relationship works

★ if you understand what is happening when it starts to go wrong

★ if you have learnt the skills which help a marriage to work well.

This book gives every couple ways to improve their chances of making marriage work for them. For those who are marrying in church and want to know where God is in all of this the book also suggests where to look.

'How can any book help us to improve our chances of a successful marriage? We know our own business best'.

This was the attitude of the five different couples described at the end of this introduction. Yet all of them agreed to go on a journey of discovery. They agreed to look at the processes underlying every married relationship, to learn how a marriage works.

Each couple wanted to check the theory against their own experience, to see if it helped them to understand their unique relationship. At the end of their journey all ten individuals agreed that

★ they had discovered a lot about themselves

★ they understood their partner better

★ each couple was more aware of the way they got on together, and how to change this if they wanted to

★ the journey itself had been interesting and enjoyable.

INTRODUCING THE 'MARRIAGE WORKS' FLOWCHART

This book is written for couples about to marry. You can share some of the stages in this journey to discover how a marriage works. There are pieces to read, quizzes to complete, ideas to consider, opinions to discuss, other couples' experience to think about. A pencil and some paper are all you will need to try out some of the exercises for yourselves: they are marked with this symbol

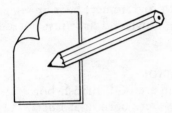

Other exercises simply ask you to talk to each other. They are marked like this

A marriage is not a 'thing out there'. It is yourselves and the way you interact. This interaction is constantly changing, sometimes moving along well-worn tracks, sometimes taking new paths. As you make your way through this book you will find that a flowchart describing this interaction is gradually built up. The flowchart is developed from an idea thought out by two Americans called Sherwood and Glidewell. Bit by bit it describes how a marriage comes into being, how it works and when it doesn't.

You stake a lot upon your intention to create a good life together. Working through this book together can help you to change intention into power.

THE FIVE COUPLES

These are the five couples whose journey of discovery you can share.

Jen and Stuart
Jen 24 and Stuart 26 have known each other for three years. She is a computer programmer; he is an engineer. They now feel ready to settle down and have just put a deposit on their first house.

Laura and Winston
Laura and Winston are both British-born. Her parents came from Trinidad, his were born in St Lucia. He has had several jobs but is not in work at the moment; she is a teacher with plenty of ambition. They are getting married because each needs the other.

Samantha and Gary
Samantha and Gary have been together for six years. They have a large group of friends who enjoy going to the seaside at weekends on their motorbikes. Now they want to start a family and have agreed to get married because that will give a baby greater security.

Jock and Glenys
Jock is a Catholic from Scotland and Glenys was brought up as a Welsh Presbyterian. They share many interests and would like to face life together. He is an electronic engineer and she gets out a catalogue for a chain store. The Welsh language is very important to her, whereas the Catholic religion means a lot to him.

Jim and Marion
Jim (21) and Marion (18) have known each other all their lives. Both were baptized as Catholics, although this means

more to their families than it does to them. She works in a bank, is keen on clothes and is good with colours. He is skilled at painting and decorating.

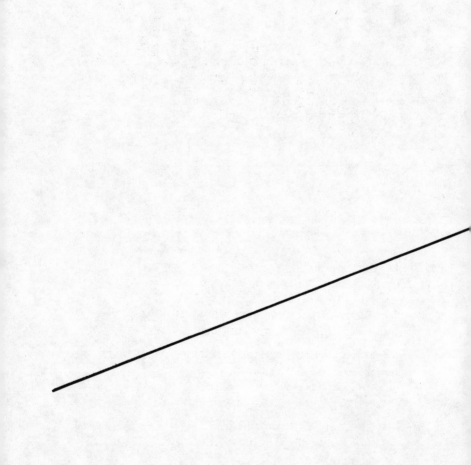

PART ONE

Could it work?

Lord, you examine me and know me
you know if I am standing or sitting
you read my thoughts from far away
whether I walk or lie down you are watching
you know every detail of my conduct.

It was you who created my inmost self
and put me together in my mother's womb
for all these mysteries I thank you:
for the wonder of myself, for the wonder of your works.

You know me through and through
from having watched my bones take shape
when I was being formed in secret
knitted together in the limbo of the womb.

from psalm 139

TWO DIFFERENT BACKGROUNDS

ASSUMPTIONS
NEEDS
FEARS
TALENTS

ASSUMPTIONS
NEEDS
FEARS
TALENTS

A personal relationship between any couple begins when from two different backgrounds each starts to show an interest in the other and to share something of themselves. As they get to know each other better these different backgrounds have much to contribute to the quality of the relationship. By the time a couple are planning to marry they usually know each other's history and temperament quite well and are aware that these affect the way they get on together. The next few pages focus on your different backgrounds.

ARE YOU TAKING A LOT FOR GRANTED?

We all do. We couldn't function otherwise. Sometimes it's as though we are programmed to behave in one way rather than another. Where do they come from, the programmes that tell you what to take for granted? Some you have thought out carefully, but what about the others? And what happens if your partner doesn't share them—whose programme is more important when you're choosing to work together? Try these two short quizzes:

SO THAT'S WHERE IT COMES FROM!

Sharing their replies to these quizzes helped our five couples to know themselves a bit better, and to understand their partners more clearly. They began to see where their different programmes were coming from.

Marion thought she deserved promotion but kept getting passed over. After the WHAT SORT OF PERSON quiz she and Jim talked about her unwillingness to take risks. Instead of teasing her he went through step by step how he would apply for upgrading at work. Marion realized she was quite capable of applying successfully for promotion and she got the job.

Jen and Stuart often quarrelled about the way they should spend a day together. Each thought their own plan would work better. After the TWO CHILDHOODS quiz they realized in a new way that his father made most decisions at home, whereas her mother was the more decisive partner. No wonder it felt 'right' to each of them that they should make the decisions and their partners should fall in line. No wonder they each felt hurt when their partner did not comply. The next time they planned a day together it was with more understanding and willingness to negotiate.

Has the original reason for one of your habits changed? If so, do you want to go on acting in the same way, or would you prefer to do something differently? Can you change the tape that gives you that particular programme?

WHAT DO YOU WANT FROM YOUR PARTNER?

These are the replies of the five couples who were soon getting married. Write down the numbers of any you agree with.

1 *Jen:* someone to 'tell the day' to

2 *Gary:* a partner who accepts all of me, good or bad

3 *Winston:* one person who really cares whether I live or die

4 *Stuart:* someone I can trust who won't let me down

5 *Marion:* a partner I can feel safe with

6 *Samantha:* another human being who thinks I'm the tops

7 *Jim:* one person who will spell the word 'home' for me

8 *Jock:* someone who will have sex with me and mean it

9 *Samantha:* a partner who will enable me to have children

10 *Glenys:* a partner who enjoys life and wants to share it

11 *Stuart:* a partner to help me achieve all I intend to do

12 *Laura:* someone to gladden the heart and set the pulse racing

If you picked out any of the numbers 1 to 12 it means you need something from your partner. That's fine. We all have needs. In spite of this, it's sometimes quite hard to tell your partner you want something from them. Yet it's great to know you're needed. How will your partner know this if you don't tell them?

Here's something to try. Look back at numbers 1 to 12 above. Choose one you agree with, and try telling your partner about it. For instance, if you agree with number 4, try saying to your partner 'I need you because you are someone I can trust and rely on, who won't let me down'. After you've both had a turn, try to say the same thing to each other in your own words.

After this it will probably be easier for each of you to think of another need you have, not listed above, which you hope your partner will meet. Have you ever told your partner this? How about each of you trying now?

IT SCARES ME

On the next page you will find three statements which describe other people's marriages. Next to each is a fear often felt by couples about to marry. Turn the page and spend a few minutes thinking whether that same feeling ever scares you as well. Try telling your partner how you feel.

If you're never scared, even a little, could you be taking too much for granted? Most people whose partner is beginning to mean a lot to them are afraid of losing what they have come to value. Yet you'll never succeed at relating well if fear of failing stops you trying.

It is possible to learn to relate better than many people do. Some of the skills you'll need are on pages 18 to 25.

Other people's marriages

We get a lot of couples in here for an evening meal. You can tell the married ones. They never have anything to say to each other.

Restaurant waiter

Father used to drink. Mother used to nag. She'd shout at him. He'd hit her. We children were all relieved when he left and they got divorced. And I think, they used to love each other once, just like the two of us.

Girl, engaged to be married

I worshipped my brother. He took me fishing, showed me everything I know. Then he started going out with this girl. They're married now. And he's trapped. Can't go out with the boys. Can't go anywhere without asking her. Can't even go fishing.

Young man

It scares me that our relationship might become boring, dull routine. That we could end up taking each other for granted.

I feel this:

- [ ] a lot
- [ ] sometimes
- [ ] a little
- [ ] never

It scares me that if I really fall in love I could be hurt, let down, abandoned or betrayed.

- [ ] a lot
- [ ] sometimes
- [ ] a little
- [ ] never

It scares me that if I get into a committed relationship I might lose my freedom.

- [ ] a lot
- [ ] sometimes
- [ ] a little
- [ ] never

YOU ARE THE SUNSHINE OF MY LIFE

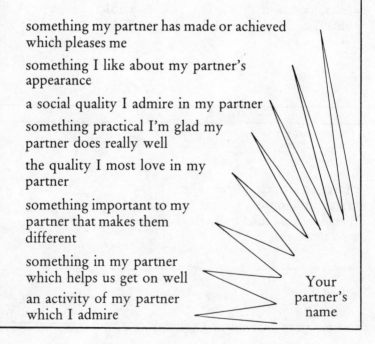

Marriages are built upon a combination of the partners' talents. How long is it since you praised each other for some of the good things each brings to your relationship? Here's a simple exercise in counting your blessings. Just draw a sunburst, write in it your partner's name, and draw eight rays from it. At the end of each sunray fill in relevant qualities which you like in your partner.

something my partner has made or achieved which pleases me

something I like about my partner's appearance

a social quality I admire in my partner

something practical I'm glad my partner does really well

the quality I most love in my partner

something important to my partner that makes them different

something in my partner which helps us get on well

an activity of my partner which I admire

Your partner's name

Here is the way Jock completed his sunburst:

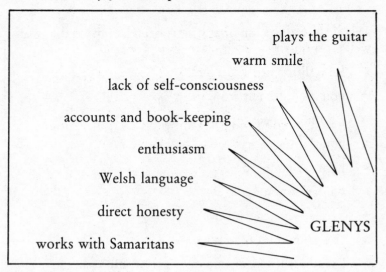

Glenys's sunburst was like this:

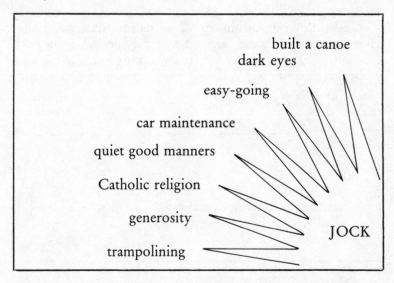

When Jock and Glenys explained their sunbursts to each other it was like stepping out of the shadow into the sunlight. Each felt capable and each felt valued. Try it for yourselves.

RESPECT

This is the foundation of any personal relationship that works well. It means that both partners understand

★ I am different from you

★ you are different from me

★ I do not expect you to be like me

★ you do not expect me to be like you

★ I am on your side

★ you are on my side

★ I trust your capabilities

★ you trust my capabilities

★ I will not force, shame or nag you into changing

★ you will not force, shame or nag me into changing.

Looking at the different backgrounds which any couple bring to a personal relationship can help them to understand why their partners are as they are and why they behave as they do. The exercises you have completed so far are likely to increase your understanding of each other. From such an understanding respect can grow.

> Do you receive a proper respect from your partner? Try telling each other about a way in which you feel respected and a way in which you would like to be respected better.

THE FLOWCHART STARTS TO MOVE

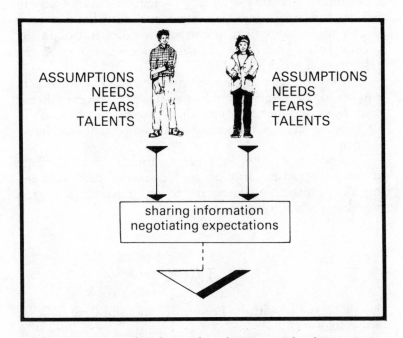

ASSUMPTIONS
NEEDS
FEARS
TALENTS

ASSUMPTIONS
NEEDS
FEARS
TALENTS

sharing information
negotiating expectations

Any new personal relationship begins with the partners taking an interest in each other and being ready to reveal something of themselves. At first the revelations are likely to be relatively impersonal—common interests and hobbies, the weather, news and politics. As a couple get to know each other better they are likely to share much more of their inner world, their feelings, loves and hates, their anxieties and pleasures, their hopes and fears. By the time the couple are planning to marry they usually know and understand each other well, but if their relationship is truly alive they will continue to volunteer information about how they think and feel from day to day, and how they react to changing circumstances.

As well as this self-disclosure, couples will also begin to sort out what they expect from each other. They may start by agreeing when and where to meet, and how they will spend their time together. Later they will have a range of expectations based on their experiences together, on what choices they have made and how they have sorted out past disagreements. If they are ready to marry they are likely to have reached a state in which they can ask for what they want with a good chance of their partner providing it, can predict accurately a whole range of each other's behaviour and can rely on each other a good deal.

If at any point during this self-disclosure and negotiation of expectations a couple do not like what they discover or do not find their needs met, they may choose to end the relationship. Otherwise their continuing relationship will inevitably deepen.

The next few pages look more closely at how to share information satisfactorily by appropriate self-disclosure and by skilful listening. They are followed by ways to test whether a relationship is genuine.

I-TALK

Don't be stingy with it. Personal relationships are built on self-disclosure.

Don't save it up then dump it all over your partner. Let it suit the time, place and person.

React to events as they happen, and use it to share your reactions.

Let it be about feelings as well as events.

Expect it to get deeper with time.

Take a few risks. Being understood at a deeper level makes the risk worthwhile.

If your partner is open with you, make sure you're equally honest in return.

Don't use it to hurt your partner but to show how you yourself feel.

Practise in turns by reading out the sentences in the bubbles to your partner and completing them honestly. Don't think for too long: try to be spontaneous.

Something I don't like about myself is. . . .

It makes me jealous when. . . .

I feel hurt when——

I daydream that. . . .

When you disagree with me I. . . .

I'm really happy when. . . .

I get angry if. . . .

I am scared of. . . .

Something I'm a bit ashamed of is. . . .

I wish I was able to. . . .

It makes me excited that. . . .

Something I've often wanted to tell you is. . . .

HOW DO I KNOW YOU'RE LISTENING?

Here is an exercise Samantha and Gary tried. Samantha spent two minutes telling Gary about something important that had happened to her that day at work. Gary tried to listen as well as he could, WITHOUT SAYING ANYTHING AT ALL.

What did Gary discover? 'It was very difficult. I kept fighting the urge to butt in, to ask questions or to say how I felt about it. I didn't seem to be contributing at all'.

How did Samantha feel about it? 'Oddly enough, Gary gave me a lot just by letting me tell the story in my own way. He was alert, he watched me closely, he nodded and grunted to show he understood. I definitely felt listened to'.

Giving your partner time to tell the story without interruption.
Holding back the questions and comments.
Listening with your whole body.
These are the first skills of good listening.

Try this exercise in silent listening for yourselves. See what you discover. First one of you speaks for two minutes and the other gives them full attention, but without speaking. Then try it the other way round.

THE MUSIC BEHIND THE WORDS

The next exercise Gary and Samantha attempted went a bit further. This time Gary gave the two minute talk, telling Samantha about an elderly man who complained loudly about young people today being work-shy scroungers. Samantha tried to listen as before, and then to respond by saying how Gary felt about the man's behaviour. Samantha hesitated. Angry? Aggressive? Misunderstood? Samantha caught the twinkle in Gary's eye, heard the laugh in his voice.

'Amused!' she ventured. 'You felt amused. A bit regretful, too, I think'.

'Spot on', said Gary. 'Hey, it feels great to think you know me so well'.

> Take it in turns for one of you to talk for two minutes about something quite important. The other gives non-verbal encouragement, then responds by saying which feeling seemed uppermost in their partner's account. The first speaker tells them how near they came.

Picking up a person's feelings and checking if you've caught them right conveys understanding better than anything else. Far better than asking questions about the facts. It's called listening with empathy. It's indispensable to partners who want to grow in understanding.

ARE YOU GENUINE?

You can't feel at home in a relationship unless you are expressing yourself honestly within it. You may intend to be genuine, but does that get across to your partner? One way of finding out is for each of you to look at the pairs of opposites listed on page 25, and to decide for each pair how near to the left or the right your partner's behaviour towards you usually is.

Jot down the letters a to j and write beside each the number which most corresponds to your partner's usual way of relating to you. Then share the results. Don't spend too long in thought: the numbers you choose are only a rough guide. The benefit comes from talking about the way each partner's efforts to be genuine actually come across. But it's worth adding up your scores and seeing if the appropriate comment applies to you.

WHEN WITH ME MY PARTNER

a	remains him/herself	5 4 3 2 1	acts a part
b	at ease	5 4 3 2 1	guarded
c	spontaneous	5 4 3 2 1	programmed
d	open	5 4 3 2 1	defensive
e	lets me be	5 4 3 2 1	on the attack
f	willing to share	5 4 3 2 1	silent and secretive
g	straightforward	5 4 3 2 1	devious
h	consistent	5 4 3 2 1	unpredictable
i	trusts me	5 4 3 2 1	tries to contradict me
j	gives honest feedback	5 4 3 2 1	gives false reassurance

SCORE

40 to 50 You usually manage to be yourself even when you're with your partner. Keep on trying to be genuine, and remember to be caring as well.

30 to 40 Can you be thinking 'If my partner knew me better he/she wouldn't like me'? Isn't it worth trying for a relationship where you are both known AND liked?

10 to 30 Either you're not really serious about giving yourself to this relationship or you are very afraid of hurting or being hurt. Can you and your partner agree to be a bit tougher for the sake of being genuine? You're both probably a lot stronger than you think.

For a personal relationship to be healthy and grow there is no substitute for

REG	OR RUBY
Respect	Respect
Empathy	Understanding
Genuineness	Being
	Yourself

REG and **RUBY** are what a man and woman look for when upon their first attraction they start to build a personal rapport.

This is what encourages them to know each other better and to become a steady couple.

This is what they seek to make lasting when they decide to marry.

Instinctively they know that **REG** and **RUBY** are needed to satisfy the human heart, and are at the root of good, satisfying married love.

If you have worked through the exercises in Part One you will already have improved your **REG** and **RUBY** skills.

GETTING IN DEEPER

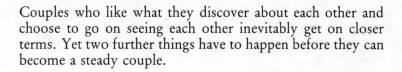

Couples who like what they discover about each other and choose to go on seeing each other inevitably get on closer terms. Yet two further things have to happen before they can become a steady couple.

CLARIFYING ROLES

Gary: You'll come to the match on Saturdays and I'll go shopping with you on Thursday evenings.
Jen: You can rely on me to talk to your parents twice a week if you stay for a weekend once a month with mine.
Jim: If I bring us a take-away every Wednesday, will you fix a hot meal for us on Friday nights?
Laura: I'll write letters for both of us if you'll help out at the old people's evenings.

These are all examples of couples clarifying roles. The partners learn to rely on each other for certain regular arrangements, usually on a tit-for-tat basis.

> Try listing some of the roles you are each taking on at the present stage of your own relationship.

COMMITMENT

Without this there is no really personal relationship.
Commitment can be of differing degrees.

A   *at the start of a relationship*
    I want a share in your joys
                            sorrows
                            worries
                            interests
                            responsibilities

B   *a comfortable and familiar couple*
    For the time being I share your joys
                                    sorrows
                                    worries
                                    interests
                                    responsibilities
                                    and they are important
                                    to me.

C   *a very committed couple*
    Now and always I share your joys
                                sorrows
                                worries
                                interests
                                responsibilities
                                and they are as important
                                as my own.

If you are planning to marry you are probably
moving somewhere between B and C. See if your
partner agrees.

STABILITY

When a couple are agreed about their roles and have some degree of commitment their relationship will enter a period where everything seems stable.

PART TWO

How it works

My beloved is mine and I am his.

Set me like a seal on your heart,
like a seal on your arm.
For love is strong as death,
jealousy relentless as Sheol.
The flash of it is a flash of fire,
a flame of the Lord himself:
Love no flood can quench,
no torrents drown.

The song of songs

Part One has explained the steps a couple go through to reach a relationship with some degree of commitment. For the time being everything's fine.

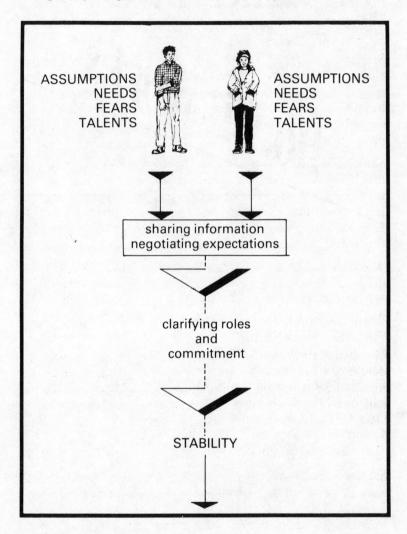

ASSUMPTIONS
NEEDS
FEARS
TALENTS

ASSUMPTIONS
NEEDS
FEARS
TALENTS

sharing information
negotiating expectations

clarifying roles
and
commitment

STABILITY

A stable relationship is a joy and a delight
It is for this that people give up part of their independence. This gives them a centre, a goal, a meaning. A feeling that all is well.

Stability in a relationship can never last long

Inevitably, inexorably, there comes a PINCH.
Pinches are experienced by one partner.
The other wonders what all the fuss is about.
Here are examples of some pinches:

Stuart has come to rely on **Jen** going with him to a health club on Tuesdays and Thursdays. Lately Jen has sometimes stayed late at the office owing to pressure of work and Stuart has had to go to the club on his own. Now Jen says she can never be free on club nights if she wants to be considered for promotion.

Samantha took a lot of trouble buying a sweater for **Gary** to match his best trousers, but he never seems to wear it. He turned up recently at her friend's party in a torn shirt and old jeans. Samantha says they will soon have no friends left if Gary doesn't smarten up. Gary shrugs his shoulders and says real friends will take them as they are.

Winston is proud of **Laura** and likes to be seen with her at discos and parties. Lately she has insisted on leaving early, saying she has to get up for work the next day. Winston suspects that she doesn't really like his friends or their way of enjoying themselves.

Marion and her mother have spent long hours planning the details of their wedding and reception, but Marion finds **Jim** increasingly bored with the whole affair. Now Marion has had a row with her chief bridesmaid and all Jim can say is 'That's one fewer for next month's charade.'

'This is not how it should be'

Stuart, Samantha, Winston and Marion are all feeling some kind of PINCH. The pinch is made worse because Jen, Gary, Laura and Jim can't see any reason for distress. As far as they're concerned, everything's as fine as it ever was.

Maybe you wouldn't feel these particular pinches, but sooner or later all relationships come to a pinch. The solid line in the diagram indicates that periods of stability inevitably end in a pinch.

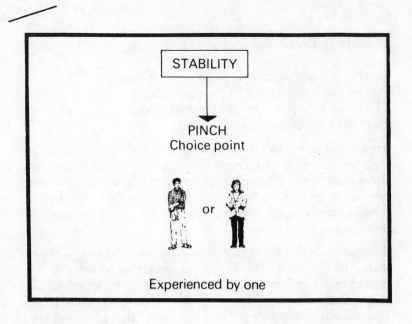

STABILITY

PINCH
Choice point

 or

Experienced by one

What was the last pinch in your relationship?
Is one of you feeling a pinch right now?

RESOLVING PINCHES: WHAT CAN I DO?

1 'It's not really happening'

One way of dealing with a pinch is to ignore it. Pretend all is well and go on as though nothing had happened. Most people do this with pinches at first, hoping they'll go away by themselves.

The snag is that this doesn't work. If nothing happens to change the situation by chance, the person feeling the pinch is condemned to go round in an endless circle:

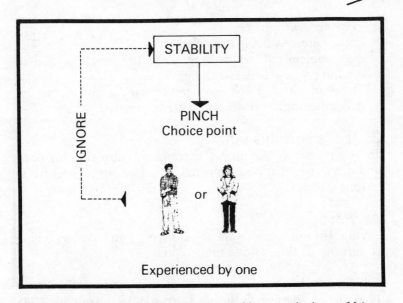

STABILITY

IGNORE

PINCH
Choice point

or

Experienced by one

Stuart will still feel Jen thinks more of her work than of him; Samantha will still resent Gary's scruffy appearance; Winston will still suspect Laura looks down on him and his friends; and Marion will still feel Jim doesn't care enough about the wedding that means so much to her.

All the time they feel victims, the situation seems out of their power to control. There has to be a better way of dealing with pinches than ignoring them.

2 'We still love each other anyway'

Another way to cope with a pinch is to deal with it indirectly. Stuart could lose no opportunity to remind Jen of all the fun she is missing at the club. Samantha might start joking at Gary's appearance, showing him up in front of friends and hoping he gets the message. Winston could begin to pick on Laura: 'You're too grand for reggae, I suppose. Beethoven more your style?'. Jim could buy Marion a bunch of flowers and give her a big hug saying 'We still love each other, don't we?'. Any of these indirect methods might resolve the pinch. But they have two drawbacks:

They are ambiguous.
Will these methods have the desired effect?
Will the other partner get the message?

They prevent growth.
Each couple is denied the chance of dealing directly with the problem, of discovering ways to resolve it and of reaching a new understanding.
The immediate pinch may be remedied, the chance of strengthening the relationship may be missed.

3 'Let's sort this out'
In any personal relationship there is no substitute for open and direct negotiation of pinches. Pinches can be negotiated in four stages.

A *Recognition*
Saying 'It's not working, is it?' Realizing you have something to sort out. Setting aside a time to do it.

B *Confrontation*
Here the person feeling the pinch has to take the initiative. He or she must explain what the trouble is. This is not a licence to accuse or blame your partner. 'You don't care about our wedding. You don't care about me! You NEVER try to see things my way!' is not likely to get Marion's pinch resolved. A more constructive (if elaborate) approach would be:

> Jim, *I know* you're good at making practical suggestions once you put your mind to something. *When you refuse* to help me solve my disagreement with Susan *I feel* let down *because* I rely on you to help me keep my sense of proportion.

This confrontation has several parts

★ it starts by affirming Jim. Marion points out one of Jim's good qualities which they are going to need in resolving the pinch

★ it goes on to say precisely what behaviour of Jim's is hurting Marion

★ it says how Marion feels

★ it explains why

Working out a confrontation like this can help you to practise how to confront effectively. Try to change the following ineffective attempts into confrontations that take the form NAME + AFFIRMATION + WHEN YOU... I FEEL... BECAUSE... Just jot your version down on a piece of paper. Then compare versions with your partner and try to agree which would work best.

Stuart: You're just a hard-faced career woman. You don't put half the energy into our life together that you put into that damned office!

Samantha: You really take the prize for Britain's best dressed man!

Winston: Do you think my friends might get the idea that you leave early because you're too grand for them?

When you've done that you may like to put these confrontations into your own words. Unless Marion and Jim usually communicate in long speeches, Marion is more likely to say something simple like

'Jim, You're the practical one. I can't sort this on my own. Please help me.'

Try writing Stuart's, Samantha's and Winston's confrontations more simply, but remember to keep them as effective as your more elaborate versions.

C *Responding to confrontation*

If your partner is brave enough to confront you about a pinch, you need to know a way of responding that will help to resolve it. The first two steps of an effective response you have already worked on. They are

★ listen

★ say how you think your partner is feeling. A feeling response from Jim would be 'You're feeling betrayed because I seemed glad at your row with Susan'.

★ clarify the problem. Because pinches are by definition felt by one partner only the confrontation may appear to come out of the blue. Find out more about the behaviour complained of and the feelings that it arouses. If you're upset at the confrontation say so, but show that you're willing to understand the pinch. Jim discovered that Marion thought he was being uncaring and unsupportive.

★ say how the situation strikes you. Jim had thought Marion was overwrought and unreasonable.

★ acknowledge that there's a mutual problem: you and your partner see the same situation differently. Remember what was said on page 18 about RESPECT. Both partners think their wedding is important, but Marion thinks this should be demonstrated by elaborate ritual whereas Jim thinks something simpler would be more in keeping. The pinch affecting one partner is now replaced by a problem affecting them both. At last they can set about solving their mutual problem.

D *Problem solving*

In the best solutions

★ both gain something, which is known as **WIN-WIN**
(Jim gains a simpler wedding, Marion solves the bridesmaid problem)

★ the goal is *Achievable*
(not 'we'll have a wedding day without any stress and strain' but 'we'll have a wedding with stress and strain minimized')

★ the goal is *Behavioural*—it is agreed that somebody does something
(not 'let's not worry about the bridesmaids' but 'let's agree to ask Susan to be the chief bridesmaid and to take charge of the smaller bridesmaids for us')

★ the goal is *Measurable*—it's clear enough to know whether it is achieved or not
(as in 'Let's ask Susan to assemble the bridesmaids, rehearse them in their duties, check their dresses, teach them to ask her for any help they need and to report to us on her progress')

★ the goal is *Worthwhile*
(a wedding with minimum hassle is a worthwhile goal, one that is perfectly straightforward but rides roughshod over other people's expectations is probably not).

A way to remember all this is by the phrase **WIN A BMW**.

Try to devise solutions to Stuart's, Samantha's and Winston's pinches which meet the **WIN A BMW** criteria. Jot down your solutions and compare them.

To summarize, pinches are best resolved by

A Recognition
B Confrontation
C Response
D Problem solving.

Couples completing this process will find themselves going anew through all the familiar procedures of sharing information, negotiating expectations, clarifying roles and commitment, until they reach a new stability.

The way all personal relationships work is shown on the flowchart. Remember: there is no substitute for open and honest negotiation of pinches.

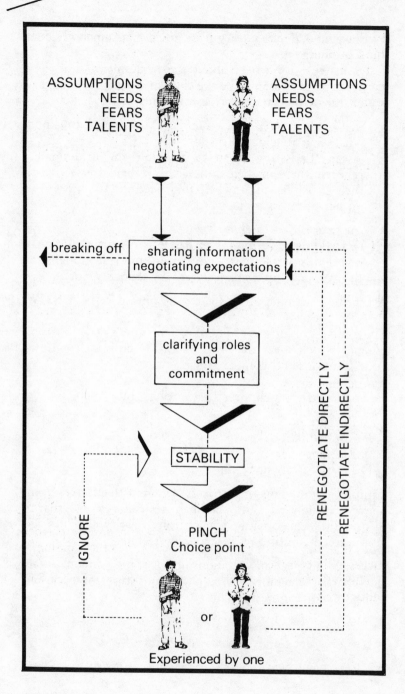

ASSUMPTIONS
NEEDS
FEARS
TALENTS

ASSUMPTIONS
NEEDS
FEARS
TALENTS

breaking off

sharing information
negotiating expectations

clarifying roles
and
commitment

STABILITY

RENEGOTIATE DIRECTLY

RENEGOTIATE INDIRECTLY

IGNORE

PINCH
Choice point

or

Experienced by one

By the time any man and woman reach the stage where they think of marrying they will have been round the circle of

    stability————pinch---renegotiate---stability

many, many times. If they choose to marry they will go round the circle hundreds of times more.

    Marriage is a dynamic relationship, always on the move. Its stability is ever temporary, constantly challenged by changes in the couple's external situation and within the couple themselves. A pinch demands adjustment in the face of changing circumstances.

COPING WITH A PINCH

Pinches are uncomfortable but they are points of choice and of growth.

Ways of coping with pinches that don't seem to work are

★   ignoring them

★   soldiering on

★   bearing them bravely

★   putting up with them

★   'offering them up'

★   sacrificing oneself

★   trying to solve them alone.

All these are admirable in other circumstances. Why don't they work in a marriage? This has to do with the commitment to be a couple, which is weakened every time one partner 'goes it alone' but is strengthened every time renegotiation is successfully completed.

    The MARRIED way of showing self-sacrifice, bravery and endurance is

★   to *recognize* that a marriage is not working well

★   to *confront* one's partner with that truth

★   to *respond* positively to confrontation, and

★ to *solve* the mutual problem.

Sometimes this takes more courage than soldiering on alone. It certainly shows more commitment to the relationship.

PINCHES ARE GROWTH POINTS

When one partner feels a pinch in a marriage it helps to know that this is entirely to be expected. There is no need to panic, to feel 'things shouldn't be like this'. A couple will have negotiated many past pinches successfully to reach a stage where they were ready to marry.

Pinches are inevitable. If the marriage stays alive and vital one or other partner will continue to feel pinches from time to time until death parts them. A pinch is a signal that a marriage is ready for further growth.

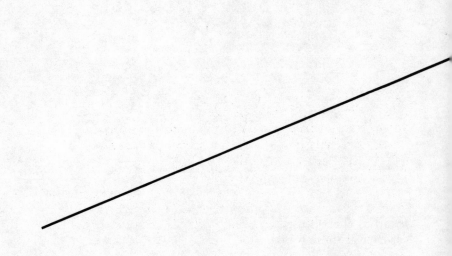

PART THREE

When it doesn't work

God is our shelter, our strength
ever ready to help in time of trouble
so we shall not be afraid when the earth gives way
when mountains tumble into the depths of the sea
and its waters roar and seethe,
the mountains tottering as it heaves.

from psalm 46

Does a woman forget her baby at the breast
or fail to cherish the son of her womb?
Yet even if these forget
I will never forget.

Isaiah 49

In marriages where there is both parental approval of the marriage and good family relations after the wedding, then there will be important support for the newly-weds.

from *Who divorces?* by Barbara Thornes and Jean Collard

IMPROVE YOUR CHANCES

It's natural to be nervous as your wedding day comes near. But have you anything to be scared about?

Research shows that some marriages have a low risk of running into trouble. If you know you are one of these couples it can give you courage. Other couples take a higher risk. If you are among these, it is best to face up to the particular danger and take steps to improve your chances.

These are some reasons which make people think twice about marrying. It's worth sitting quietly on your own and writing down the number of any which might apply to you. Then read the comments on page 48 to see how to improve your chances.

1 All these wedding preparations are getting me down. Sometimes I wonder if I really do want to get married. But how can I get out of it now?

2 He says I bring him luck. I only wish that horse hadn't run off with so much of our savings.

3 We've only known each other for a few months but I know we're going to be very happy.

4 I love him but I wish he didn't drink so much.

5 They say teenagers are too young to know their own minds, but I know our love will last for ever.

6 She can't bear me out of her sight. If I so much as speak to another girl at a party it's nag, nag, nag for the rest of the evening.

7 We're getting married in a Catholic church to please her mum. Of course, neither of us are practising Catholics, but at least that way we're marrying for keeps.

8 He's always getting into fights. I used to try and drag him away, but then he started on me. Now I just walk away. He says marriage will cure him.

9 My girl says if I ever leave her she'll kill herself. She's already taken an overdose several times. I'm really sorry for her but I'm beginning to feel blackmailed.

10 Our wedding will be a case of East meets West. We've overcome problems of family, religion, background and race. The problems of marriage will be easy after this.

11 She used to go with another bloke, in fact I know they had sex together. All that's in the past. But last week we had a silly row and she finished up spending the night with her ex-boyfriend. She says she'll be faithful once we're married.

12 With a baby on the way the best thing we can do is to get married as soon as possible.

13 I was heartbroken when my first engagement was broken off. Who would have thought that four months later I would be getting married to somebody else? This time it's for ever.

Short engagement
3 and 13   If you have known each other for only a short time you are taking a risk getting married so soon. Love at first sight is possible, but needs to be tested over time. This is especially so if you're on the rebound from a broken relationship. Some people say it's best to let a year go by before committing yourself again.

Stormy courtship
2 4 6 8 and 11   If you are always having rows, maybe you don't have enough in common to make a happy marriage. If you love your partner enough to show that you can change habits of gambling, jealousy, drinking or promiscuity beforehand your marriage stands a much better chance than if you expect getting married to cure these problems by magic.

Young or pregnant
5 and 12   Teenage marriages *can* last, especially where both sets of parents help out. But the divorce figures show that marrying under twenty is riskier than for over twenties. This applies even more if the wife is pregnant.

Church wedding
7   Unfortunately, marriages of people belonging to a religion in name only break up as often as other people's. But those who practise their religion are less likely to divorce.

Mixed marriage
10   Marriages *do* succeed across religious, cultural and racial divisions. But it's a lot harder to understand things your partner takes for granted. Make sure that you both mean the same thing when you say you want to be married.

Not sure
1 and 9   Lots of people feel scared of the wedding day but certain of their partner. If it's your partner you're unsure of or who's making all the running, then think carefully. Nobody can decide you want to marry except you yourself.

'Divorce will never happen to us'
The risk will be less if none of the thirteen situations apply to

you or your partner before you marry. Yet nobody enters marriage nowadays without realizing that marriage today is a high-risk undertaking.

Marriage today is fragile
One marriage in three ends in divorce. As you approach marriage you can take some comfort that two married couples out of three actually choose to stay together. If you want to do something practical to improve your chances further it is worth looking clearly at what happens when a marriage starts to go wrong.

Are couples the victims of this fragility?
Married couples are not helpless in the face of marriage breakdown. The rest of Part Three explains what happens when a marriage begins to go wrong. By making the effort to understand this thoroughly you will see what has to be done to avoid real danger for your marriage. Start by returning to the 'Marriage Works' flowchart page 40.

What happens when pinches are ignored?
When one partner in a marriage starts to feel that something is amiss, it was explained in Part Two that the quickest way back to stability is honest and open negotiation. Pinches can also be sorted out in less direct ways and eventually stability can be restored. It is when pinches are habitually ignored that the relationship is in real danger. New stability is feigned but nothing has really changed. The pinch continues to be felt.

WHATEVER HAPPENED TO REG AND RUBY?

There follows a period of increasing unhappiness and exasperation. Rows may become frequent, and be bitter and destructive. Behaviour becomes unpredictable, as couples thresh about trying first one tactic and then another to restore equilibrium. Genuineness is an early casualty, as couples find themselves playing elaborate roles, intent on scoring points rather than reaching an honest understanding. In short, **REG** and **RUBY** (page 26) seem to have deserted the married couple.

'What are you playing at?'

'What on earth do you want?'

'It's not fair!'

'There's no pleasing you!'

'You make me furious!'

Eventually they reach a CRUNCH:

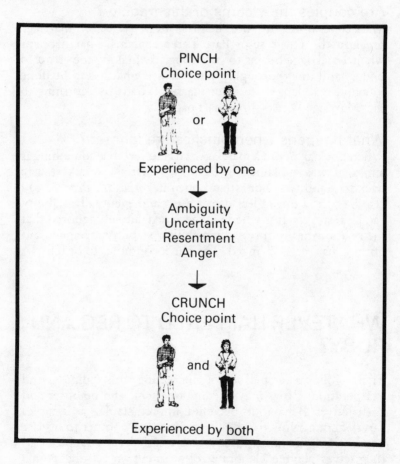

PINCH
Choice point

or

Experienced by one

↓

Ambiguity
Uncertainty
Resentment
Anger

↓

CRUNCH
Choice point

and

Experienced by both

WHAT IS A CRUNCH LIKE?

The expression CRUNCH is used to describe an intolerable situation where both husband and wife know that something is seriously awry between them. Each seems to provoke the behaviour they cannot bear. Perhaps she nags because he comes home late, while he comes home late because she nags. Or, he neglects her because she drinks while she drinks because he neglects her. Or, she is sexually unresponsive because he is violent while he is violent because she is unresponsive sexually. So wife and husband are locked into an ever-worsening spiral. They seem unable to help themselves. They have reached the CRUNCH.

'It's all a mess!'

'We're destroying each other!'

'Whatever can be done?'

GETTING OUT OF A CRUNCH— THREE UNSUCCESSFUL WAYS

1 'Let's forget the past and start again'
Most couples try to get out of a crunch by new resolutions, especially at first, saying 'Let's start behaving like a proper husband and wife again. Let's turn over a new leaf'. Sadly, resolutions by themselves change nothing and sort nothing out, so the course is set for a return to pinch and again to crunch.

2 'We'll stay together but it's all over really'
Whether they stay for the children's sake, or for security or for appearances, some couples come to accept that their marriage is emotionally dead. Spontaneity, mutuality, growth together in love, these are no longer possible for them. All that is left is a grey co-existence.

3 'It's all over and I'll get my own back in the divorce court'

Sadly, some couples can find no way of ending an intolerable crunch except by separating permanently or divorcing. These divorces are notable for the rancour, ill-will and vengefulness of the negotiations.

SO HOW CAN A COUPLE GET OUT OF A CRUNCH?

'Let's make one last effort to sort this whole mess out'. Many marriages have been to the crunch, to breaking point, and have recovered. It is difficult, because negotiations start under such stress. Sometimes a couple need a skilled helper, such as a marriage counsellor, to hold the ring for them. A good counsellor can prevent them from destroying each other, can help them to understand what has been happening between them, and can ease them through the many small recognitions, confrontations, responses and solutions which are needed before they can start to understand each other again and plan for the future.

With or without skilled help, there is no guarantee that the marriage can be salvaged. If a couple cannot recover some commitment to each other then they may agree to divorce or separation. Conciliators or counsellors can help them to settle this constructively and without rancour, so that each may take up a new life with the least possible damage.

RETURNING TO COMMITMENT

The hope is that a couple may sort out their differences well enough to build a future together. Honest talk and generous listening will help them agree new roles, to commit themselves not to the past but to the present and the future.

The full pinch-crunch flowchart is reproduced on the next page. It shows how a marriage works, and what happens when it doesn't. Understanding this is an important step towards improving your chances of a working marriage. Help each other now to run over the whole flowchart, tracing all the possible paths a marriage can take.

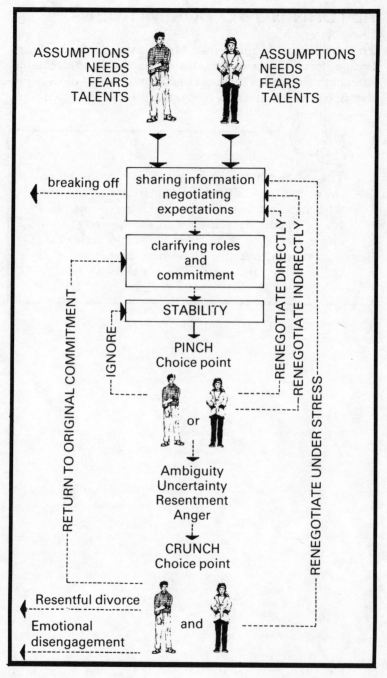

ASSUMPTIONS
NEEDS
FEARS
TALENTS

ASSUMPTIONS
NEEDS
FEARS
TALENTS

breaking off

sharing information
negotiating
expectations

clarifying roles
and
commitment

STABILITY

PINCH
Choice point

or

Ambiguity
Uncertainty
Resentment
Anger

CRUNCH
Choice point

Resentful divorce

Emotional
disengagement

and

RETURN TO ORIGINAL COMMITMENT

IGNORE

RENEGOTIATE DIRECTLY

RENEGOTIATE INDIRECTLY

RENEGOTIATE UNDER STRESS

REMEMBER

Pinches are inevitable.

Crunches are not.

The best way to avoid a crunch is by honestly and openly sorting out pinches. Part Four highlights some of the pinches that most couples getting married need to sort out together.

PART FOUR

Making it work

Jesus said:
So then, if you are bringing your offering to the altar and there remember that your brother has something against you, leave your offering there before the altar, go and be reconciled with your brother first, and then come back and present your offering.

Matthew 5

The couple who want to make a successful marriage commit themselves to direct negotiation of pinches. They do not promise to have no differences but they commit themselves to work constantly to reconcile the pinches that inevitably occur.

An excellent way to prepare for a successful marriage is to look at topics where many couples have different attitudes, and to practise direct negotiation. This is what the five couples whose journey of discovery you are following agreed to do. They were all fairly open and honest, yet each of them skated round certain sensitive areas.

Jen and Stuart had very different ideas about how to reconcile work and domestic roles. For a long time Jock and Glenys avoided discussing religion and family planning, while Jim and Marion steered off sexual topics and anything to do with wedding plans. Laura and Winston felt differently about getting somewhere to live and about their attitudes to children. Samantha and Gary had some unspoken resentment about their use of money and what each expected from the other.

In Part Four you can share some exercises which gave the five couples plenty of scope for practising direct negotiation of pinches. Remembering **REG** and **RUBY** (see page 26) see what the exercises have to offer you.

IN MY CHILDHOOD HOME

Do you and your partner vary in the amount of personal space that you need and the amount of closeness that seems right to you? Often such differences can be traced to the world you took for granted in childhood.

Jot down your own responses, then check with your partner whether your experiences as children were similar or very different. Maybe you will want to recognize that your partner has different assumptions from yours and to make allowances.

In my childhood home

1 we used to make jokes   often/sometimes/rarely

2 we used to touch each other   frequently/sometimes/hardly ever

3 kisses and cuddles were   normal/measured/rare

4 when people felt angry they would   hit out /row/sulk/suppress it

5 we'd discuss our plans   fully/partly/reluctantly

6 my business was   everybody's/interesting/my own

7 we prided ourselves on our   concern/interest/independence

8 nakedness was accepted/avoided/frowned upon

9 sex was discussed readily/when necessary/never

10 children were disciplined by   my dad/my mum/both/neither

11 children said prayers with   my dad/my mum/both/neither

12 we went out   together/independently/rarely

13 I liked it when my dad...

14 I liked it when my mum...

15 I was unhappy when...

SOMEWHERE TO CALL HOME

One of the biggest hurdles facing couples today is finding and affording somewhere suitable to live. Often this determines the date of a marriage and whether the marriage is viable. It is also a major joint venture which the couple undertake for each other.

The wheel opposite shows some of the efforts needed to get a home together. Try 'walking' round the wheel to see whether there is anything extra you can do together or individually to make your chances of a suitable home come a little nearer.

spend more time at DIY

save more money

register with the council

go to the housing advice centre

get friends to help

find an extra source of income

mobilize help from the family

spend more time looking at
likely places

seek professional advice

take a job with accommodation

scour house agents' ads

think about changing jobs

ask friends and workmates for information

consider another area

answer that letter, make that call

compare different building societies' terms

MAKING ENDS MEET

Taking each other 'for richer, for poorer' implies mutual trust, and agreement about what money is for and how to spend it.

This quiz is a practical start to your discussions about money. Try it separately first, then compare your answers.

1 Do you know how much each other earns or receives from other sources?

2 How will you both keep an eye on where the money goes?

3 Will you keep money in any of these places?
   Hidden at home?
   In a bank account?
   In a building society account?
   With the National Giro Bank?
   In a Post Office account?

4 Are any accounts you have in one name only or are they joint accounts?

5 How will you decide what you ought to spend your money on?

6 How do you feel about:
   Taking out a loan?
   HP?
   Regular saving?
   Life insurance?

7   Who will pay:
       The mortgage or rent?
       The rates?
       The TV licence?
       The telephone bill?
       For the holiday?
       The HP?
       The electricity and gas bills?
     Have you considered a budget account or standing orders?

8   How much money do you think you should have a week to do exactly what you like with?

9   Which of these descriptions helps describe your attitude to money?

generous	tight
careful	spend as soon as you can
happy to talk about it	not happy to talk about it
put some away for a rainy day	always save hard

10   If you have children what difference will this make to your plans?

11   If you are both in work, what would happen if one or both of you lost your job?

12   Have you made any arrangements for your partner and any family you may have in the event of your sudden death? If so, what?

13   Have you considered making a will?

ROLES AT HOME AND AT WORK

Jot down the numbers 1 to 8
Put a tick if you agree with the statement
Put a cross if you disagree
Then compare your choices with your
partner and try to say why you think as you do.

1   I would like us to divide up the household tasks in much the same way as my parents did.

2   Some jobs in the house are really women's work. If so, which?

3   It is important to work out clearly which household jobs are the husband's responsibility and which the wife's.

4   If a household job needs doing, both husband and wife should always be equally prepared to do it.

5   Wives should look for less tiring jobs than their husbands because they will be more responsible for running the home.

6   Husbands have to put more energy into their paid work than wives into theirs.

7   If my partner is out of work I will still regard him/her in the same way.

8   If I am out of work I will still value myself as much as I do now.

SEXUALITY

Marriage is a sexual relationship between a woman and a man. Sex is not the whole of the relationship but it is an important and basic part. Sexual intercourse can symbolize the entire relationship, demonstrating belonging, closeness, trust, mutual delight and giving, excitement, comfort and satisfaction. Most couples would like to talk together about sexuality in a way that is honest and trusting.

Yet it's easier to explain your attitudes to sexual matters to your partner if you have thought them through by yourself first. Try sitting alone quietly and considering the questions which follow. Use a pencil and paper if that helps. Then tell your partner anything you would like to share together.

1   What makes me feel good about being a man/woman?

2   What do I dislike about being a man/woman?

3   Which is nearest to my own attitude:
    ★ I feel good about my body
    ★ My body's not marvellous but it's OK
    ★ I think about my body as little as possible
    ★ I really wish my body were different

4   How far do I agree with these statements:
    ★ I want to share my body with my partner
    ★ I feel shy about sharing my body with my partner
    ★ It's a pity that marriage involves sharing my body with my partner

5   Sharing my body with my partner will be more satisfying or easier if...

6   When I think about my partner's body I...

7   Do I like to kiss my partner or show affection in public? Do I like my partner to do this?

8   Apart from my partner, do others of the opposite sex turn me on easily? If so, how will I cope after I am married?

9   Do people of my own sex sometimes attract me sexually? If so, how do I cope with this? and how will it affect my partner?

10 Most people have sexual fantasies, but do mine have any good or bad effect on real life for me?

11 Do I love my partner enough to admit there are things I don't know about sex? Where could we start to find out some things we need to know?

12 Where did I pick up my own first information about sex? Were my parents, teachers and friends helpful, or not?

13 Have I seen any books, films or pictures about sex which have left a lasting impression?
    Is it a happy or unhappy one?

14 Most people have had some unpleasant sexual experiences, but have I had any advances from a member of my own sex, a flasher, a groper, a rapist or a relative which still disturb me?

15 If I had sexual intercourse with others previously, is the memory largely pleasant or unpleasant? What effect will it have on my marriage?

16 After I am married, what do I most want out of our sex life together?

17 Is there any 'unfinished business' about my experiences on the way to sexual maturity that I need to sort out with a marriage counsellor, clergyman, doctor or some other trustworthy person? How could I set about doing this?

18 How much of my responses to these questions do I want to share with my partner now?

SEXUAL ROLES

Jeff and Liz have been married for nearly a year. These are some of the things they have said to each other about sex during that time.
Try telling your partner whether or not you think each statement is justified, and why.

Jeff has told Liz

Just because I still like looking at girlie magazines, it doesn't mean I don't love you.

It would turn me on a lot better if you wore more sexy underwear.

I wish you wouldn't always expect me to make the first move. Why can't *you* suggest having sex sometimes?

I want to satisfy you but I'm not sure how. Will you show me what turns you on?

I want to tell you what I'd really like us to do when we have sex but I'm afraid you'd either be shocked or laugh at me.

I love having sex with you and helping you enjoy it too. When I think that God made sex for us to enjoy each other like this it changes my whole idea of God.

Liz has told Jeff

It bothers me that other pretty girls can still get you going. Can't you realize you're married to me now?

Why can't we just kiss and cuddle sometimes? Why do you always have to go all the way?

I wish you'd realize that I have to get in the mood before I'm ready to have sex.

When we have sex, will you sometimes tell me in words how it feels to you?

When I'm lit up after we have sex, why do you always turn over and go to sleep and leave me up in the air?

Sex with you makes me feel right and reminds me who I belong with. I'm beginning to see how God gave us sex to help us become one.

CHILDREN

Write down the numbers of any points with which you tend to agree. See if your partner has the same attitude to children.

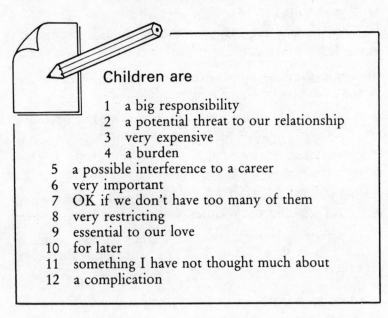

Children are

1 a big responsibility
2 a potential threat to our relationship
3 very expensive
4 a burden
5 a possible interference to a career
6 very important
7 OK if we don't have too many of them
8 very restricting
9 essential to our love
10 for later
11 something I have not thought much about
12 a complication

13 for as soon as possible
14 something we have to talk about
15 not for me
16 more the woman's decision
17 why I am getting married
18 not so important to a modern marriage
19 not something I want to concentrate on now
20 something that adds to marriage
21 fine if a person has that temperament
22 irresponsible to have in today's world
23 too much of a worry
24 a woman's responsibility
25 a man's financial burden
26 a moral obligation
27 something I want
28 something that scares me
29 a comfort for old age
30 wonderful: I want a large family
31 OK if my partner wants them
32 important to femininity
33 important to masculinity
34 important for our parents' happiness
35 for both parents to care for equally
36 what marriage is all about
37 a kind of immortality
38 a blessing
39 hostages to fortune
40 a share in creation

CHILDREN OF YOUR OWN

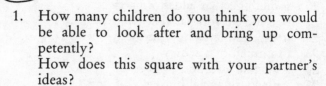

1. How many children do you think you would be able to look after and bring up competently?
   How does this square with your partner's ideas?

2. Do you agree on the best method for your own situation of preventing or spacing conception? Are you both happy that your chosen method is reliable? acceptable? moral? healthy? Where could you get trustworthy advice if you need to know more?
   When would you both like to review this decision?

3. Are you in broad agreement about when to start a family?
   What will you do if the wife gets pregnant before you both really intended?
   What could you do if starting a baby proves difficult?

GOD AND THE PRACTICE OF RELIGION

Religious faith is often called a gift. This means that you can't force yourself to believe in God or in any particular religion simply because you want to please your partner or to share their faith. Yet because a person's religious belief often changes at life's turning points it's useful when you are preparing for marriage to clarify how important God or the practice of religion is to you at the moment.

You need to check how your partner stands because religion is about the deep things of life, religious belief may be more important to your partner than you suppose.

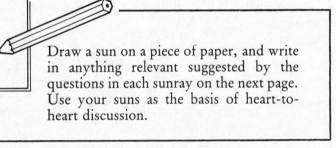

Draw a sun on a piece of paper, and write in anything relevant suggested by the questions in each sunray on the next page. Use your suns as the basis of heart-to-heart discussion.

3 TODAY
How do you see God?
How important is God to you?
How often do you go to church?
What church teachings are important to you?
What do you do differently because of your beli
Are you involved in any church activity?
When do you pray?

2 BECOMING INDEPENDENT
Periods of doubt?
      apathy?
      enthusiasm?
Church attendance?
Involvement in church life?
Personal prayer?

1 YOUR UPBRINGING
School influences?
Was God
  a kind father?
  a tyrant?
  not important?
Did God matter to father?
      to mother?
Did you go to church a lot?
      pray a lot?

5 YOUR FUTURE CHILDREN
Will you
teach them about God?
bring them for baptism?
pray with them?
expect them to attend any particular
church?

4 BOTH OF YOU
Do you
worship together?
pray together?
talk about religion?
avoid talking about religion?
base joint decisions on religious principles?
find religion a source of strength?

GOD
and the practice of religion

CELEBRATING THE WEDDING

A wedding day is the statement of many contrasting values and attitudes, the meeting point of many individual hopes and fears. Small details can carry unsuspected emotional meanings. This helps to explain why wedding plans can cause friction, like the problem Jim and Marion met about bridesmaids.

It can be good to step aside from the planning and to concentrate on yourselves. Following this book or going on a marriage preparation course can be helpful: your own relationship is more important than any detail of its celebration.

With your sense of proportion restored you will want to plan the wedding which sums up your own situation best. Marion and Jim found this exercise useful. See if completing it helps you.

1 Who has had the most influence on our wedding plans? Pick the top four:

me   you
my mother   your mother
my father   your father
my friends   your friends
         any other person.

2 We have chosen to get married in a church because...

3 One change I should like to make in our wedding plan is...

4 After our wedding the thing I should most like guests to say about it is...

5 I should really like us to be able to say that our wedding day was...

If you have worked through the exercises in Part Four and discussed your findings together you will have practised resolving pinches in all of these areas:

childhood
housing
money
work
roles
sex
children
family planning
religion
wedding plans

When you marry you commit yourself to work at this continually, daily. Marriage is a permanent commitment to a reconciling love.

PART FIVE

God works in ordinary marriages

No one has ever seen God;
but as long as we love one another
God will live in us
and his love will be complete in us.

The First Letter of John 4:12

May your blessing come upon this man and woman.
May they praise you in their days of happiness
and turn to you in times of sorrow.
May they know the joy of your help in their work
and the strength of your presence in their need.
May they worship you with the Church
and be your witness in the world.
May old age come to them in the company of their friends,
and may they reach at last the kingdom of heaven.

Adapted from the Marriage Service

THOSE SPECIAL MOMENTS

Winston: The first time I saw Laura I knew she was the girl for me. Don't ask me how, I just knew. I can't get over how lucky I am that she thinks the same way.

Glenys: When Jock said he loved me I didn't feel much emotion. But later when I was alone thinking it over, I realized what he had said.
I laughed out loud. It was great to feel loved.

Gary: The effort Samantha puts into hunting for somewhere for us to live makes me feel really grateful.
Nobody has every worked so hard for something I wanted before.

Jen: Stuart's joy when I got a good job did wonders for me. I thought he'd mind because I get more pay now than he does but he seemed really pleased for my sake. It makes me feel more confident.

Jim: We had a row and I thought the best way to make it up was by mending her old banger. She wrote me a note. It just said 'Dear Jim. Thanks for fixing my car. Love, Marion.' I knew then that it was all right between us. I've always kept that note.

Special times. Important. Significant.
Ordinary to others, they meant a lot to the five couples who were soon getting married.

Every couple has their own story, the narrative of events which are important to them alone. It's worth going over yours together, telling each other your shared history, reminding each other of the times you have shared which really matter to you both.

There is another name for what really matters in life. Christians call it GOD.

> *MARRIAGE IS*
> knowing God
> through the deep experiences
> shared by a man and a woman.

EVERYDAY LOVE

A group of married couples were asked:
'What sort of everyday help have you come to expect from your partner? What things do you rely on your partner to do for you?'
These were some replies:

making tea
buying stores
cleaning the lavatory
mending the roof
earning money
putting out the rubbish
doing the accounts
relieving sexual tension

calming me down
listening to my day
hearing my worries
making time for me
confirming my masculinity
accepting me as I am
making me laugh
reminding me of other people's feelings

planning holidays
decorating the house
encouraging me to dress well
backing my job application
making me feel great in bed
showing me how to cook
praising my talents
being proud of my achievements

Look at the three lists. First come practical services, done by one partner for the good of both. Next there are personal attention and kindness. Thirdly are ways husbands and wives encourage each other or use their talents to improve each other's lives.

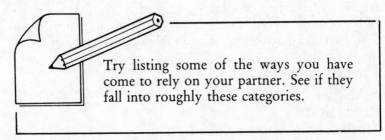

Try listing some of the ways you have come to rely on your partner. See if they fall into roughly these categories.

Dr Jack Dominian, who is a well-known expert on marriage, maintains that couples today have three purposes in getting married. In marriage they expect to
SUSTAIN EACH OTHER
HEAL EACH OTHER
HELP EACH OTHER TO GROW.
Where they achieve this sufficiently, the marriage lasts and is

successful. Where they fail, the marriage is likely to come to an end.

Look again at the three lists. Alternative headings for them could be SUSTAINING, HEALING and HELPING GROWTH. It looks as though the group of married couples who volunteered the lists would agree with Dr Jack Dominian.

How about you? Try putting S H or G after each item on your own list of the ways you have come to rely on your partner, according to whether each item sustains you, heals you or helps you to grow.

There is another name for the power which supports and sustains us.
Christians call this power God the Father.
Healing or redemption Christians see as the work of Jesus, the Son of God.
Growth is seen by Christians as the work of God's life-giving Spirit.

In the everyday examples of sustaining, healing and helping growth which ordinary married couples experience Christians can point to the presence of the Trinity, the presence of God as Father, Son and Spirit.

MARRIAGE IS
experiencing God
as Father, Son and Spirit
when husband and wife
sustain each other,
heal each other
and help each other to grow.

SHOW ME

Christians believe that God is always present in the most everyday actions of our lives. As well as this, many Christians would like to show God's presence particularly clearly at special events in a person's lifetime, such as birth, death or marriage. They recognize that God is present in the special moments and in the everyday love of couples getting married. When they celebrate the sacrament of marriage the new husband and wife make lifelong promises to each other and so become a living sign of the love of God which has no end. They exchange rings 'as a sign of love and fidelity' and so make real to their relatives and friends God's love and faithfulness which is alive and active between the two of them.

> I take you...
> to have and to hold
> from this day forward
> for better, for worse
> for richer, for poorer
> in sickness and in health
> to love and to cherish
> till death do us part.

MAKING MARRIAGE WORK

Running through the Christian story is the notion of repentance, conversion or change.
The Baptist cried
> 'Repent, for the kingdom of heaven is close at hand'.
> (Matthew 3:2)
Jesus started his preaching by proclaiming
> 'Repent and believe the good news' (Matthew 4:17)
and Peter proclaiming the risen Christ answered those who asked 'what must we do?' with
> 'You must repent'. (Acts 2:38)
The married Christian is daily called to repentance, to change and conversion, called to reconcile the inevitable pinches

before they reach crunch point. That's what this book has been about. That's what you have practised by working through the exercises. That's why you have improved your chances of a marriage that works. That's the way God will work within your marriage.

MARRIAGE IS
a permanent commitment
to a reconciling love

Notes and References

pp 11, 14, 15   The idea that we are programmed by our childhood experiences to react in particular ways comes from transactional analysis. Two simple books explaining this and much else about the hidden causes of our behaviour are: *I'm OK, you're OK* by Thomas A. Harris, published by Pan 1973; and *What do you say after you say hello?* by Eric Berne, published by Corgi 1975.

pp 20, 21   Self-esteem is vital to a successful married relationship. It prevents the partners from being over-demanding of love and reassurance. The way this can happen is described in *Marital Breakdown* by J. Dominian, published by Penguin 1968. Further exercises in self-esteem can be found in *Lifeskills Teaching Programmes* by Hopson and Scally, published by Lifeskills Associates of Leeds in 1980.

p 25   Self-disclosure is an important skill and no married relationship can get far without it. One of the best books dealing with this is from America and as with all American books it is important to translate it into our own way of speaking to get the best from it. It is *You and Me* by Gerard Egan, published by Brooks/Cole 1977.

pp 26, 27, 28   Further exercises in listening skills can be found in G. Egan op. cit., as can a discussion of genuineness.

p 32   I first heard of REG and RUBY from Jen Anderson of the Counselling and Career Department Unit of Leeds University. I have found this mnemonic useful for bringing to mind the most important skills of relating, especially as its double form makes me think about its meaning.

p 39, 40, 41   G. Egan again deals exhaustively with confrontation.

p 43   Winners and losers are concepts drawn from transactional analysis.

p 43   This terminology for goal-setting is adapted from *People in Systems* by G. Egan, published by Brooks/Cole 1979.

pp 49   'At risk' marriages are discussed in *Make or Break* by J. Dominian, published by the Society for Promoting

Christian Knowledge 1984 and research data can be found in *Who divorces?* by Barbara Thornes and Jean Collard, published by Routledge and Kegan Paul 1979.

p 58 A description of the way marriage counsellors work can be found in *The remaking of marriages* by Quentin de la Bedoyère, published by The Liverpool Institute of Socio-Religious Studies, Christ's College, Woolton Road, Liverpool L16 8ND in 1978.

p 63 Further exercises on many of the topics in part four are published in *Your Future Begins Now*, published by the Catholic Marriage Advisory Council, 15 Lansdowne Road, London W11 3AJ. Other useful exercises can be found in *Preparing for the sacrament of marriage* by Del Vecchio, published by Ave Maria Press 1980.

p 67 The 'making ends meet' quiz is reproduced from *Side by Side*, a video-based marriage preparation course published by the Church Pastoral Aid Society, 32 Fleet Street, London EC4Y 1DB.

p 69 The quiz on roles at home and at work was first published in *Water made Wine* by Margaret Grimer, published by Darton, Longman and Todd 1986.

pp 71, 72, 73 This quiz on sexuality is adapted from *Side by Side*.

p 74 The sexual roles quiz was first published in *Water made Wine* by Margaret Grimer.

p 75 Adapted from *Your Future Begins Now*, CMAC.

p 86 *Marriage, Faith and Love* by J. Dominian, published by Darton, Longman and Todd 1981.